KOI FISH

THE

A-Z GUIDE

CONTENTS

KOI FISH

THE

A-Z GUIDE

Introduction

Welcome to the world of Koi keeping. This book is a gateway into a realm that combines beauty, tranquility, challenge, and reward in equal measure. As we embark on this journey together, it's important to understand what makes Koi fish so captivating to people around the world.

The Allure of Koi Fish The Koi fish, with its vibrant colors and graceful movements, is more than just a pretty face in the world of aquatics. Originating from Asia, these creatures have become a symbol of peace, prosperity, and perseverance in various cultures. Their majestic presence and captivating patterns create a mesmerizing spectacle, making Koi ponds the centerpiece of countless gardens and spaces worldwide. But their allure goes beyond their physical charm.

Koi keeping is often described as a form of aquatic gardening. It is an art that combines the practicality of fish keeping with the aesthetics of landscape design. The act of caring for these creatures, watching them grow, and even breeding them, provides a sense of fulfillment that can hardly be paralleled.

Purpose of the Book This book is designed to be your companion in this journey. Whether you're a novice just starting, a hobbyist looking to deepen your knowledge, or an enthusiast contemplating turning your passion into a profession, this comprehensive guide aims to equip you with the knowledge you need.

From understanding the historical and cultural significance of Koi fish to exploring their diverse varieties, from setting up your first Koi pond to mastering their diet and health care, each chapter of this book is a step forward in your Koi keeping journey.

You'll also find insights into the world of Koi breeding, common problems, and their solutions, as well as a comparative look at Koi keeping vis-à-vis other beginner-friendly fish. Join us as we dive into the captivating world of Koi, exploring the depth of information beneath the surface. It's not just about fish-keeping; it's about embracing a hobby that will bring tranquility, challenge, and immense joy into your life.

Welcome to "Koi Keeping: An A-Z Guide for Beginners and Enthusiasts."

Chapter 1: Origins and Significance of Koi Fish

As we embark on the journey of Koi keeping, it's crucial to delve into the roots of these fascinating creatures. Their rich history and symbolic significance are as colorful as their radiant scales.

Historical Background

The history of Koi, known scientifically as Cyprinus rubrofuscus, traces back to East Asia, where carp species were initially domesticated for food. The term "Koi" itself is simply Japanese for "carp." However, the Koi we know today—prized for their stunning array of colors and patterns—were the product of selective breeding that began around the 17th century in Japan.

The carp, initially a dull, muted color, began to exhibit mutations with vibrant colors and patterns. The Japanese farmers of Niigata noticed these unique carps and started breeding them, selecting and cultivating the most beautiful specimens. As the generations passed, these Koi, or "Nishikigoi," as the Japanese refer to these ornamental carp, transformed into the mesmerizing swimmers we admire today.

Koi keeping began to gain international popularity in the 20th century. After a Tokyo exposition where some of the prized Koi were exhibited, interest in these stunning creatures grew. Today, Koi are kept in ponds worldwide and are considered a symbol of beauty, tranquility, and perseverance.

Symbolism

The Koi fish holds profound symbolic meanings in different cultures, most notably in Japan and other parts of Asia. Considered a swimming metaphor for human life's aspirations, Koi are associated with various positive qualities.

In Japanese culture, Koi are symbols of love and friendship due to their peaceful nature and graceful, synchronized swimming. Furthermore, Koi are known for their longevity and resilience, symbolizing perseverance and the ability to overcome obstacles, reflecting the belief that one can "go against the current" to attain life's goals. Their ability to swim upstream is associated with the Boys' Day Festival in Japan, where they represent the desire for boys to grow into strong, determined men.

In Chinese culture, the legend of the Dragon Gate tells of a Koi that swam upstream, through waterfalls and rapids, to become a dragon upon reaching the top of the mountain. This tale positions Koi as a symbol of ambition, courage, and the ability to attain high goals.

Through their historical journey from food to admired ornamental pets, Koi have swum into the hearts of people worldwide. Their rich symbolism adds depth to their aesthetic appeal, rendering Koi keeping an enriching experience transcending the boundaries of a simple hobby. As we delve deeper into the world of Koi, these aspects add layers of appreciation for these fascinating creatures.

Chapter 2: Types of Koi

The world of Koi is a kaleidoscope of colors, patterns, and sizes. While they all share the common characteristics of grace and beauty, different types of Koi have unique features that make them distinct. Understanding these types is essential for any Koi enthusiast.

Overview

At first glance, Koi might seem similar, but a closer look reveals an array of differences. There are over a hundred varieties of Koi, each with unique coloration, patterns, and scalation. These varieties are the result of centuries of selective breeding, resulting in the diverse collection of Koi we have today.

The types of Koi are broadly classified into categories based on their color, patterns, and type of scales. Some of the well-known categories include Gosanke, Hikarimuji, Hikarimoyo, Kawarimono, and Tancho. Within these categories, there are specific varieties that Koi keepers and breeders recognize and appreciate.

In-Depth Look

As we explore each type in detail, you'll learn to appreciate the diversity that exists within the world of Koi. Each variety has its unique charm and beauty. We'll explore each type's unique characteristics, complete with detailed descriptions and vivid photos, which will serve as your guide to understanding and identifying Koi types.

For instance, in the Gosanke category, we have three major types: Kohaku, Sanke, and Showa. Kohaku are white Koi with red patterns, representing the simplicity and elegance that is deeply appreciated in Japanese aesthetics. Sanke Koi are primarily white with red and black markings, while Showa are black Koi with red and white patterns, known for their bold, striking appearance.

Beyond these, there are metallic Koi like the Hikarimuji and Hikarimoyo varieties, and the unique, 'one-of-a-kind' Koi in the Kawarimono category. Then there are the Tancho Koi, unique for their singular red spot on the head, a pattern that reminds one of the Japanese flag.

This in-depth exploration will not only deepen your understanding of Koi varieties but also sharpen your eye for detail. As a Koi enthusiast, this knowledge will enhance your appreciation for the beauty and uniqueness of each fish, adding more depth to your Koi keeping journey.

Kohaku

Kohaku is one of the most popular types of Koi and is included in the "Big Three" or Gosanke, which also includes Sanke and Showa. Kohaku Koi are white-bodied fish with red (or hi) patterns. The white color should be a pure, milky white, while the red should be deep, like the color of a bright red apple or the Japanese flag. The pattern of red on the white body varies greatly from fish to fish. A high-quality Kohaku often has a balanced and well-defined hi pattern.

Sanke

Sanke, also known as Taisho Sanshoku, is another type of Koi in the Gosanke. The Sanke Koi is primarily white-bodied with both red and black markings (sumi). The red pattern should be evenly distributed across the body, while the black spots, which are usually smaller, can appear on top of the red markings or on the white skin. In general, a good Sanke has a strong contrast between the colors, and the boundary lines between each color should be clear and sharp.

Showa

Showa, also known as Showa Sanshoku, is the third type of Koi in the Gosanke. Showa Koi are characterized by a black body with both red and white markings. Showa Koi are known for their showy, striking color patterns. Unlike Sanke, the black color in Showa Koi is not just limited to spots but can cover larger portions of the body. An ideal Showa has a balanced pattern of black, red, and white.

Hikarimuji

The term Hikarimuji encompasses all Koi that are a single, metallic color. One of the most popular types in this category is the Ogon. An Ogon is a Koi of one solid color, and it can be various colors, such as white (Platinum Ogon), yellow (Yamabuki Ogon), and orange. Their entire body has a metallic sheen, and their unpatterned body gives a simple, elegant appearance.

Hikarimoyo

Hikarimoyo includes all Koi with two or more metallic colors. One common type is the Hariwake, which displays a pattern of solid, vibrant yellow or orange combined with a bright metallic white. The contrast between the colors is often sharp, and the patterns vary greatly, making each Hariwake unique.

Kawarimono

Kawarimono is essentially a category for Koi that don't fit into any other category, including many different colors, patterns, and scalation types. One of the most recognized types in this category is the Chagoi. The Chagoi is a solid-colored Koi that ranges from olive green to brown. Despite their relatively drab color, Chagoi are often beloved by hobbyists for their friendly and sociable disposition, often being the first to feed and thus encouraging shyer Koi to do the same.

Tancho

Tancho Koi are not a separate variety, but rather any Koi that has a single red dot on its head. The rest of the body is typically white. The name Tancho comes from the Japanese crane which has a similar color pattern. The red spot, which ideally is symmetrical and located right in the center of the head, represents the Japanese flag. Tancho Kohaku, Tancho Sanke, and Tancho Showa are all very popular among hobbyists.

Chapter 3: Getting Started with Koi Keeping

Keeping Koi is a rewarding experience, but like any hobby, it requires careful thought and planning. It's crucial to consider your resources, commitment, and the unique needs of Koi fish before setting up your first pond.

Initial Considerations

Stepping into the world of Koi keeping means committing to cost, time, effort, and the right environment for your Koi.

Cost: The initial cost includes setting up a proper pond, purchasing the Koi, and the ongoing costs of feeding and caring for them. Keep in mind that Koi are not just any fish; they are a premium breed that often comes with a higher price tag.

Time: Koi require regular feeding, and their pond needs to be maintained and monitored for cleanliness, temperature, and oxygen levels.

Effort: Expect to learn about water chemistry, dietary needs, disease prevention, and treatment. It's more than just feeding them daily; it's about ensuring a healthy and suitable environment.

Space: Koi are large fish that grow quite sizable and they need a spacious pond to thrive. Unlike a small fish tank, a Koi pond is a substantial addition to your home or garden.

Comparing Koi with Other Beginner-Friendly Fish

When compared to other beginner-friendly fish like goldfish, guppies, or bettas, Koi keeping can be a bit more challenging, but also rewarding.

Cost: Koi are more expensive to purchase and maintain compared to most beginner-friendly fish. The costs associated with creating a suitable habitat (pond, filtration system, etc.) are also higher.

Upkeep: Koi require more careful management of their environment than most fish. Factors like water temperature, pH levels, and oxygen levels need to be monitored and maintained.

Lifespan: Koi can live for decades, even surpassing human lifespans in some cases. This makes them a long-term commitment, unlike many other fish species that have much shorter lifespans.

Size: Koi grow much larger than typical aquarium fish. They require more space to swim and grow, which is why they are kept in ponds rather than tanks.

Interaction: One of the joys of Koi keeping is their interactive nature. Koi quickly recognize their caretakers and often come to the surface to greet them. This level of interaction is not common in many other species of fish.

While Koi keeping comes with its unique set of challenges and requirements, the rewards are immense. Their beauty, longevity, and interactive nature make Koi one of the most captivating aquatic pets one can keep. As you journey through this guide, you will uncover more insights into the world of Koi and understand why they have enamored hobbyists and collectors worldwide.

Chapter 4: Setting up Your Koi Pond

Setting up your Koi pond is an exciting venture. It's your Koi's home, and its design and maintenance will greatly impact your Koi's health and happiness. Therefore, careful planning and execution are crucial.

Location and Size

First and foremost, select a suitable location for your pond. It should be a spot that's partially shaded, as Koi aren't fans of constant direct sunlight, which can also promote algae growth. However, it shouldn't be under heavy tree coverage as falling leaves can decay in the water, affecting water quality and clogging filters.

The size of your pond directly affects the number and size of Koi you can keep. As a rule of thumb, a typical hobby-grade Koi will need a pond that holds a minimum of 1,000-2,000 gallons of water. However, larger is always better when it comes to Koi ponds. A depth of at least 3 feet is also recommended, as it allows

Koi to escape surface-level temperature fluctuations and potential predators.

Necessary Equipments

Your Koi pond isn't complete without the necessary equipment to maintain a healthy environment for your fish.

Filtration Systems: A good filtration system is crucial for keeping the water clean and safe for your Koi. It should include both mechanical filtration to remove solid particles and biological filtration to break down harmful waste products.

Aeration Systems: Oxygenation is vital for your Koi's health. An aeration system, such as a fountain, waterfall, or air stones, will ensure that your Koi have the necessary oxygen levels they require.

Heating Elements: Depending on your local climate, you may need a heating system to keep water temperatures stable, particularly during colder months. Koi thrive at temperatures between 59 and 77 degrees Fahrenheit.

UV Sterilizers: UV sterilizers are useful in controlling algae growth and eliminating harmful bacteria and parasites that could cause disease.

Safety Measures

Keeping your Koi safe from predators and disease is a major aspect of Koi care.

Predator Prevention: Netting can prevent birds or cats from attacking your Koi. If you have a problem with raccoons or other similar predators, a steep and deep pond design can prevent them from reaching the fish.

Disease Prevention: Maintaining good water quality, a balanced diet, and a stress-free environment for your Koi is the best disease prevention. Additionally, quarantine any new fish before introducing them to your pond to prevent the spread of potential diseases.

Setting up your Koi pond is a project that requires planning, investment, and a fair amount of work, but seeing your Koi swimming happily in its well-designed environment makes it all worthwhile. Your pond is the foundation of your Koi-keeping journey, and a well-set-up pond will make the journey smoother and more enjoyable.

Chapter 5: Koi Diet and Nutrition

A well-rounded diet is fundamental to your Koi's growth, color, health, and longevity. Unlike many fish species, Koi are omnivorous, and their diet can and should include a mix of proteins, carbohydrates, and plant matter.

Balanced Diet

High-quality Koi food: Commercially available Koi food is designed to provide a balanced diet to your Koi. These foods often come in the form of floating pellets, which allow you to observe your Koi feeding - a good opportunity to check for signs of good health or potential problems. Look for food that has a high protein content (at least 30-40%) and includes essential vitamins and minerals.

Vegetables: Koi can eat a variety of vegetables, including lettuce, watermelon, peas, and oranges. Vegetables can be a great source of vitamins, and many Koi enjoy them. Make sure to wash all vegetables thoroughly and cut them into small, manageable pieces.

Insects and larvae: Insects and their larvae are a natural food source for Koi and can provide valuable protein. Some Koi keepers like to supplement their Koi's diet with insects like silkworms, mealworms, or even commercially raised shrimp.

Feeding Schedule

The amount and frequency of feeding your Koi depend on the water temperature, as Koi metabolism is affected by the temperature of their environment.

During warmer months when the water temperature is above 60 degrees Fahrenheit, Koi have a high metabolism and should be fed 2-3 times per day. In contrast, when the temperature drops below 60 degrees, their metabolism slows down, and they should be fed less frequently.

Feed only what your Koi can eat in about 5 minutes, and avoid leaving uneaten food in the pond, as it can degrade water quality. Young Koi can eat a larger amount of food relative to their body weight, while adult Koi eat less.

Adjusting the diet according to the seasons is also necessary. In summer, a high protein diet is essential to support Koi's active metabolism, whereas in winter, a low protein, high carbohydrate diet is recommended.

Remember, overfeeding is one of the most common mistakes in fishkeeping. Overfeeding can lead to poor water quality and health problems for your Koi, so it's important to feed them in appropriate amounts.

Your Koi's diet and feeding schedule play a vital role in their overall health and vitality. By providing a balanced diet and following a sensible feeding schedule, you'll support your Koi's health and enjoy their vibrant colors and energetic swimming for many years.

Chapter 6: Health and Disease

Just like any other pet, Koi are susceptible to a range of health issues and diseases. Early detection, prevention, and appropriate treatment are key to maintaining the health of your Koi.

Common Diseases

Koi are hardy fish, but they can fall prey to various bacterial, parasitic, and viral diseases. Some of the most common include: *Ichthyophthirius Multifiliis* (Ich or White Spot Disease): This parasitic disease is characterized by white spots on the skin, gills, and fins. Koi may exhibit signs of discomfort like rubbing against objects. Treatments include increased water temperature, salt baths, and commercial treatments.

Koi Herpes Virus (KHV): A highly contagious and lethal disease. Symptoms include gill mottling, lethargy, loss of appetite, and excess mucus production. Unfortunately, there's no known cure for KHV. Prevention is the best approach, involving strict quarantine protocols for new fish and maintaining good water quality.

Fin Rot: A bacterial infection that leads to the fraying or discoloration of fins. It's often a result of poor water quality or injury. Treatment involves improving water conditions and possibly administering antibacterial treatments.

Parasites: Koi are susceptible to various parasites, including flukes and anchor worms. Signs can include scratching, visible worms, inflammation, and lethargy. Treatments vary depending on the specific parasite and may include medicated baths or direct medication.

Regular Health Checks

Routine observation is the first line of defense in maintaining the health of your Koi. Familiarize yourself with your Koi's typical behavior, so you can quickly notice any changes.

Physical check: Look for changes in your Koi's color, fins, scales, and eyes. Check for spots, patches, cloudiness, or wounds.

Behavioral check: Keep an eye on your Koi's swimming patterns and appetite. Changes could be an early indication of potential health issues.

Water quality check: Regular testing of water parameters like pH, ammonia, nitrite, and nitrate can help prevent many health problems. Aim to test your water at least once a week and after any significant changes like the addition of new Koi or after treatments.

Annual health check: Consider bringing in a professional or a vet specialized in fish to do an annual health check-up, especially for high-value Koi.

Keeping Koi healthy involves vigilance and care. It's crucial to provide a well-maintained environment, balanced diet, and routine health checks to keep them at their best. When problems arise, early detection and treatment can make all the difference. In this rewarding journey of Koi keeping, nothing compares to the satisfaction of maintaining a healthy and thriving Koi pond.

Chapter 7: Breeding Koi

Breeding Koi can be a rewarding aspect of Koi keeping. Not only can it be a fascinating process to observe and participate in, but it also offers the chance to create new generations of beautiful Koi.

However, it's important to understand that breeding Koi can be challenging and requires a deep understanding of Koi behavior, biology, and the necessary conditions for successful spawning and growth of fry.

Understanding Koi Breeding

Koi typically become sexually mature and ready to breed when they are about 3 years old and around 10 inches long. Koi breeding is highly dependent on water temperature, with spawning usually occurring in the spring when the water temperature consistently stays between 65-70 degrees Fahrenheit.

During breeding, the male Koi will chase and bump the female to encourage her to release her eggs. Once released, the male fertilizes the eggs. It's important to note that Koi are not parental fish -

they do not care for their eggs or fry. In fact, Koi will eat their eggs and offspring if given the opportunity.

Therefore, once spawning has occurred, the eggs (which will stick to surfaces) must be separated from the adults. The eggs will hatch into Koi fry within 4-7 days, depending on the water temperature.

Spawning

Spawning is the process by which fish reproduce. In the context of Koi fish and many other species, it involves the release of eggs by the female and the fertilization of those eggs by the male.

Here's a more detailed breakdown of the process:

1. Preparation and Conditioning

Prior to spawning, Koi are often 'conditioned,' which means they are provided with a diet rich in proteins to prepare them for the energy-intensive process of reproduction. This also ensures the production of healthy eggs and sperm.

2. Spawning Behavior

When water temperatures reach an optimal range, usually between 65-70 degrees Fahrenheit for Koi, spawning behavior commences. Males will begin to chase the females around the pond. This is not just a mating dance but a crucial part of the process. The chasing and bumping stimulate the females to release their eggs.

3. Egg Release and Fertilization

The female Koi will release thousands of tiny eggs that adhere to various surfaces like plants, rocks, or special spawning brushes placed in the pond for this purpose. After the female has released her eggs, the male Koi will release sperm, or 'milt', into the water, which fertilizes the eggs.

4. Post-Spawning

Once the eggs are laid and fertilized, they should be separated from adult Koi, as Koi will eat their eggs and their own offspring. The fertilized eggs will hatch into Koi fry within 4-7 days, depending on the water temperature.

5. Raising Fry

Koi fry are very small and delicate. They will need to be fed a diet appropriate for their size, such as infusoria or brine shrimp, until they are large enough to eat regular Koi food.

In general, spawning is a complex process that requires careful preparation and monitoring. The water quality, diet, and even the specific Koi chosen for breeding can all significantly impact the success of the spawn and the health of the fry.

Tips for Successful Breeding

Successful Koi breeding requires meticulous preparation and careful observation. Here are some tips and common mistakes to avoid:

Conditioning Your Koi: Prior to the breeding season, both male and female Koi should be in optimal health. A diet rich in protein can help prepare Koi for breeding.

Creating a Spawning Environment: Spawning mops or brushes, which the eggs can stick to, should be placed in the pond. These can be removed once the eggs are laid to keep them safe from the adults.

Selecting Breeding Koi: Not all Koi are created equal, and if you're looking to breed, it's important to choose high-quality Koi with desirable traits. You can select for color, pattern, size, or any trait that you find attractive.

Maintaining Water Quality: Good water quality is crucial for the survival of eggs and fry. Regular testing and necessary adjustments are key to successful Koi breeding.

Feeding Fry: Koi fry need a special diet for their first few weeks of life. Newly hatched brine shrimp are a common food for Koi fry.

One of the most common mistakes in Koi breeding is insufficient preparation, both in terms of the Koi's health and the pond environment. Additionally, poor water quality and feeding practices can lead to a high mortality rate among the fry.

Breeding Koi is not a venture to be taken lightly. It requires time, resources, and a great deal of knowledge. However, the rewards can be great, both in terms of the beauty of the new Koi and the satisfaction of having successfully bred them.

Chapter 8: Understanding Koi Behavior

Observing and understanding the behavior of your Koi is one of the many joys of Koi keeping. It can provide insights into their health and well-being, and strengthen your connection with your fish. Below, we delve into common Koi behavior patterns and their interactions with other fish species.

Behavior Patterns

Koi have a range of behaviors that can signal different states of health, mood, and environmental conditions.

Feeding Behavior: Healthy Koi are typically enthusiastic eaters. They will rise to the surface and can even be trained to take food from your hand. If a Koi is suddenly not interested in food, it might be a sign of stress or illness.

Swimming Patterns: Normal Koi behavior includes leisurely swimming around the pond. If Koi are darting around rapidly, jumping out of the water, or rubbing themselves against objects, they may be stressed or suffering from parasites.

Gasping at the Surface: If Koi are spending a lot of time at the surface appearing to gasp for air, this could indicate a lack of oxygen in the water or a potential problem with water quality.

Floating or Sinking: If Koi are unable to maintain their buoyancy, floating at the surface or sitting at the bottom of the pond, this may indicate a swim bladder issue.

Grouping Behavior: Koi are social fish and they often swim in groups. However, if they're clustering in a particular part of the pond, it might indicate an issue with water temperature or quality in other parts of the pond.

Interaction with Other Fish

Koi are generally peaceful and can coexist with a variety of other pond fish. However, it's essential to consider the size and temperaments of different species, as well as their environmental needs.

Goldfish: Goldfish are a common companion for Koi, as they share similar environmental needs. However, Koi grow larger than most goldfish and can outcompete them for food.

Plecostomus: Often known as "plecos" or "algae eaters," these fish can coexist with Koi and help control algae in the pond. However, they prefer warmer water than Koi, so this must be taken into account.

Orfe: These are active, fast-swimming fish that can add variety to your pond. Orfe are generally compatible with Koi, but they prefer cooler water and require high oxygen levels.

One key point to remember when mixing species is that Koi can grow quite large and have been known to eat smaller fish. Always consider the full grown size of your fish when populating your pond.

Understanding your Koi's behavior and their interaction with other fish species can greatly enhance your Koi keeping experience. By watching for changes and understanding what is normal behavior, you can ensure that your Koi remain healthy and happy in their environment.

Chapter 9: Long-term Care and Overwintering

Koi keeping is not just a hobby but a long-term commitment. Koi can live for several decades with proper care, and they require specific care strategies as they age and with seasonal changes, particularly in winter.

Seasonal Changes

Seasonal changes can have a significant impact on the care of your Koi. As the weather changes, so too do the needs of your Koi.

Spring: As the water temperature begins to rise in spring, your Koi will become more active. It's a crucial time to check for any signs of illness that may have developed over the winter. Also, gradually reintroduce a regular feeding schedule as their metabolism increases with the warming water.

Summer: Summer is typically a straightforward time for Koi care, but be mindful of water temperature spikes and potential algae blooms, which can deplete oxygen in the pond.

Fall: As temperatures start to drop, reduce the feeding frequency and switch to a lower protein food. It's also the time to prepare your pond for winter, removing fallen leaves and debris to prevent decay and potential water quality issues during winter.

Winter: Koi go into a state of semi-hibernation during winter. They require very little, if any, feeding as their metabolism slows dramatically. However, maintaining good water quality is still essential, and measures should be taken to prevent the pond from freezing over entirely.

Overwintering

Caring for Koi during winter requires special consideration, especially in regions with harsh winters. Koi are cold-water fish, but they can't survive in a pond that's frozen solid. A part of the pond's surface must be kept open to allow gas exchange, preventing the build-up of harmful gases from decaying material and fish waste.

Pond heaters or de-icers can be used to keep an area of the pond from freezing. Additionally, aeration devices can help maintain oxygen levels in the water. It's also essential to monitor water quality during winter, even though Koi are less active.

Aging Koi

Just like people, Koi can require additional care as they age. Older Koi might become more susceptible to diseases and health issues. Regular health checks become increasingly important as your Koi age.

The dietary needs of older Koi can also change. They may benefit from foods that are easier to digest or those specifically formulated for older fish. Adjustments to the pond environment, like providing areas with slower water flow or more hiding spots, can also help accommodate older Koi.

Long-term Koi care involves adjusting to the changing needs of your Koi throughout the year and as they age. It's a commitment that requires understanding, patience, and adaptability. But the reward is a vibrant, thriving Koi pond that provides years of enjoyment and a meaningful bond with these captivating creatures.

Chapter 10: Common Mistakes and How to Avoid Them

Keeping Koi is a rewarding hobby, but it is not without its challenges. Here, we'll outline some of the common mistakes that beginners often make and provide strategies for avoiding them, helping to ensure your success and enjoyment in the world of Koi keeping.

Overstocking the Pond

One of the most common errors made by beginner Koi keepers is overstocking their pond. Koi need a lot of space to grow and thrive; they can reach lengths of up to 3 feet and require a significant amount of water to maintain good health. Overcrowding can lead to inadequate filtration, reduced oxygen levels, and increased disease transmission.

Prevention Strategy: Always consider the mature size of your Koi when determining how many you can keep. A general rule of thumb is to have a minimum of 500 gallons of water for the first Koi and an additional 250 gallons for each subsequent Koi.

Poor Water Quality

Maintaining good water quality is critical for the health of your Koi. Many beginners underestimate the importance of regular water testing and monitoring. Poor water quality can lead to a host of health problems, including stress, disease, and even death.

Prevention Strategy: Implement regular water testing as part of your Koi care routine. Monitor for pH, ammonia, nitrite, and nitrate levels, and make necessary adjustments to maintain optimum water conditions.

Inadequate Filtration

Koi produce a significant amount of waste, which can quickly degrade water quality without a proper filtration system. An inadequate filtration system is a common mistake that can lead to multiple problems down the line.

Prevention Strategy: Invest in a high-quality filtration system suitable for your pond size and the number of Koi you intend to keep. A good system will include mechanical and biological filtration to effectively remove waste and maintain a healthy ecosystem.

Improper Feeding

Feeding Koi may seem simple, but mistakes in feeding can lead to health issues. Overfeeding can cause poor water quality and obesity in Koi, while underfeeding can lead to malnutrition.

Prevention Strategy: Feed your Koi a balanced diet in the right quantities. This can vary depending on the season, the temperature of the water, and the size and age of the Koi. In warmer months, Koi can be fed multiple times a day, but in colder months, their metabolism slows, and they may need little or no food.

Ignoring Health Issues

New Koi keepers might not recognize the signs of disease or distress in their fish until it's too late. Ignoring or missing the signs of health issues can have serious consequences.

Prevention Strategy: Educate yourself about common Koi diseases and their symptoms. Regularly observe your Koi for any changes in behavior, eating habits, or appearance.

Avoiding these common mistakes can help ensure a healthier and happier life for your Koi. Remember, Koi keeping is a learning experience, and everyone makes mistakes. The key is to learn from them and continually seek knowledge to improve your Koi keeping skills.

Not Preparing for Predators

Predators can be a significant threat to your Koi. Birds, raccoons, cats, and even other larger fish can see your Koi pond as an easy meal.

Prevention Strategy: Use netting or similar covers over your pond, particularly if you live in an area with many potential predators. Provide places for your Koi to hide in the pond, like underwater caves or densely planted areas. Some people also use decoys or scare devices to deter predators.

Not Planning for Weather Extremes

Especially in regions with harsh winters or hot summers, failing to prepare for extreme weather can be disastrous for your Koi.

Prevention Strategy: In cold climates, consider using a pond heater or de-icer to prevent the pond from freezing solid, and ensure part of the pond is at least 3 feet deep so the Koi can hibernate below the ice. In hot climates, provide shaded areas to help keep the water temperature down, and consider using a water chiller if extreme heat is common.

Using Tap Water without Treatment

Tap water often contains chlorine or chloramines, which are harmful to Koi. Simply filling your pond from the hose can unknowingly introduce these harmful substances.

Prevention Strategy: Always use a water conditioner when adding tap water to your pond. These conditioners are designed to neutralize chlorine and chloramines, making the water safe for your Koi.

Skipping Quarantine for New Fish

Adding new fish directly to your pond without a quarantine period can introduce diseases and parasites to your existing Koi population.

Prevention Strategy: Always quarantine new fish for at least two to four weeks. Monitor the new arrivals for any signs of disease or distress before introducing them to your main pond.

Remember, Koi keeping requires knowledge, patience, and dedication. But with careful planning and attention to detail, you can avoid these common pitfalls and ensure a healthy and enjoyable environment for your Koi.

Chapter 11: Koi Vs. Other Beginner-Friendly Fish

Koi are undoubtedly beautiful and captivating creatures, but are they the best choice for everyone? This chapter provides a comparative analysis of Koi and other beginner-friendly fish, helping you make an informed decision about which species suits your lifestyle, interest, and resources best.

Introduction

The world of fish keeping offers an impressive variety of species to choose from. Each comes with its unique needs, characteristics, and charm. This chapter aims to compare Koi with other beginner-friendly fish, providing insights into factors like cost, lifespan, care needs, tank/pond requirements, feeding, breeding, and susceptibility to diseases.

Factors for Comparison

Choosing the right fish is about more than just looks. It's important to consider:

Cost: This includes the price of the fish, their habitat, food, equipment, and ongoing maintenance costs.

Lifespan: How long can you expect your fish to live under proper care?

Care Needs: What are the specific care requirements for the fish? Do they require specific water conditions, diet, or other special attention?

Tank/Pond Requirements: What kind of environment do these fish need to thrive? How much space do they need?

Feeding: What do these fish eat, and how often do they need to be fed?

Breeding: How easy or difficult is it to breed these fish?

Disease Susceptibility: How prone are these fish to diseases? What common diseases should you look out for?

Individual Comparisons

Next, we'll compare Koi to several popular species among beginner aquarists: Goldfish, Betta fish, Guppies, and Swordtails. Each comparison will highlight the pros and cons of keeping each species from a beginner's perspective.

Goldfish: Often seen as the quintessential beginner fish, Goldfish share many similarities with Koi, but they are generally smaller and have lower maintenance needs.

However, they still produce a lot of waste and require a larger tank or pond than what many beginners realize.

Betta Fish: Known for their vibrant colors and flowing fins, Betta fish are relatively easy to care for and can live in smaller aquariums.

However, they are not as social as Koi and often must be kept alone due to their aggressive nature.

Guppies: Guppies are small, colorful, and relatively easy to care for, making them popular among beginners. They reproduce easily, but their small size makes them a potential target for larger fish.

Swordtails: Swordtails are lively and colorful fish that are relatively easy to care for. They get along well with other peaceful fish but may not have the visual impact that Koi or even Goldfish provide.

Koi are a somewhat more advanced choice. They require more space, maintenance, and initial investment compared to many other beginner-friendly fish. However, they make up for it with their impressive size, longevity, and striking beauty.

Choosing Koi might be an excellent idea for beginners who are ready to invest time and effort into a rewarding hobby. Still, it might be more challenging for those looking for a low-maintenance pet. In the end, the choice comes down to your personal preferences, resources, and commitment.

Chapter 12: Designing and Landscaping a Koi Pond

Creating a Koi pond is not just about digging a hole and filling it with water. It involves a careful balance of aesthetics and functionality, designed to mimic the Koi's natural habitat and create a visual centerpiece for your outdoor space. This chapter delves into the design and landscaping aspects of a Koi pond.

Fundamentals of Pond Design

Designing a Koi pond starts with an understanding of the basic requirements for Koi health and then integrating those needs with an eye for aesthetic appeal. A successful Koi pond design should consider the following factors:

Size and Depth: Koi ponds should be deeper than the average garden pond to allow Koi enough space to grow and swim freely. They also need depth to help them escape predators and extreme temperatures.

Shape: While the shape of the pond can cater to personal preferences and the available space, smooth, curved lines often mimic natural bodies of water and create better water circulation.

Placement: Consider a location that gets partial sunlight and is free from falling leaves or other debris.

Landscaping

Landscaping around your Koi pond enhances its beauty and creates a natural, serene environment for the fish. The choice of plants, rocks, water features, and other elements should be made considering both aesthetics and the safety of the Koi.

Plants: Aquatic and marginal plants not only add to the natural look but also provide shade and help maintain water quality. However, avoid plants that are toxic to Koi.

Rocks and Gravel: These add to the natural look of the pond, provide hiding spots for Koi, and are beneficial for beneficial bacteria. However, they should be well-secured and have smooth edges to prevent injury to the Koi.

Water Features: Waterfalls or fountains add beauty and sound to your pond. They also aid in aeration, which is beneficial to Koi.

Lighting Considerations

Lighting plays a dual role in a Koi pond. It highlights the beauty of the pond and its inhabitants during the evening hours and supports the health of the pond's ecosystem.

Underwater Lighting: Underwater lights can illuminate the Koi, making them visible even after sundown. These lights can create dramatic effects in the water but should be installed safely to avoid any electrical issues.

Garden Lighting: Lighting around the pond can highlight features like plants, rocks, or waterfalls. Solar-powered lights can be an energy-efficient way to illuminate the surrounding landscape.

Biological Considerations: While Koi do not require light to sleep or wake up, plants in your pond do need light to photosynthesize and produce oxygen. Balancing the light needs of your plants and the aesthetic desires is key.

Designing and landscaping a Koi pond is a creative endeavor, allowing you to blend the needs of the Koi with your personal aesthetic preferences. With careful planning and thoughtful design, you can create a Koi pond that is both a healthy home for your Koi and a beautiful addition to your landscape.

Chapter 13: The Science of Koi Genetics

From their vibrant colors to their varying patterns and sizes, Koi fish display an impressive range of physical characteristics, most of which are the result of meticulous genetic selection over many generations. This chapter aims to provide a simplified understanding of Koi genetics and how it influences the breeding process.

Understanding Koi Genetics

At the heart of the incredible variety of Koi is genetics - the science that explains how traits are passed down from parent to offspring. A basic understanding of genetics can enhance your ability to breed Koi successfully and appreciate the complexity of the process.

Genes and Traits: Koi, like all living creatures, have genes that dictate their physical traits. These genes are segments of DNA and are passed on from both parents to the offspring. The traits we see in Koi, such as color, pattern, and size, are determined by these genes.

Dominant and Recessive Genes: Some traits are determined by dominant genes, meaning only one copy of the gene needs to be present for the trait to show. Other traits are determined by recessive genes, meaning two copies (one from each parent) are needed for the trait to be visible.

Genetic Variation: The wide variety of Koi types we see today is due to genetic variation. Mutation, a random change in genes, is the source of all genetic variation and can sometimes lead to new and desirable traits in Koi.

Selective Breeding

Selective breeding is the process of choosing specific Koi to breed based on their desirable traits. It's essentially a way of manipulating the genetic pool to increase the likelihood of these traits appearing in future generations.

Selection of Parents: The first step in selective breeding is choosing the parent fish. Breeders choose Koi with desirable traits and good health. This doesn't guarantee all offspring will carry these traits, but it increases the odds.

Breed Purity and Hybridization: Some breeders aim to maintain the purity of a specific Koi variety by breeding Koi of the same type. Others might experiment with hybridization - breeding two different types of Koi to create a unique variety.

Observation and Culling: Once the Koi spawn, breeders observe the fry as they mature. They watch for desirable traits and remove (cull) fish that don't exhibit these traits to keep the focus on the Koi that do.

Understanding and applying the principles of genetics and selective breeding can be complex but also incredibly rewarding. It has allowed breeders over many generations to develop the amazing array of Koi varieties we see today, and it remains an essential part of the ongoing journey of Koi evolution and enhancement.

Chapter 14: Troubleshooting Common Problems

Caring for Koi involves understanding and addressing various challenges that might arise, from maintaining optimal water quality to managing behavioral problems among your fish. In this chapter, we'll cover some of the common problems that Koi keepers may face and provide solutions to handle these issues.

Water Quality Issues

Maintaining water quality in a Koi pond is crucial for the health and wellbeing of your fish. Poor water quality can lead to a variety of health problems, including disease and stress. Here are some common water quality issues and their solutions:

Poor Oxygen Levels: Koi require a certain level of dissolved oxygen in the water to breathe. If oxygen levels drop too low, your fish may become stressed or even die. Installing a pond aeration system, and ensuring your pond is not overcrowded, can help maintain optimal oxygen levels.

Ammonia Buildup: Ammonia is produced from fish waste and can be toxic to Koi. Regularly testing the water for ammonia and using a biological filter can help maintain safe levels. If ammonia levels become too high, immediate water changes may be necessary.

Algae Overgrowth: While some algae are beneficial, an overgrowth can deplete oxygen levels and block sunlight. Algae growth can be controlled by limiting nutrients (like excess fish food), adding algae-eating organisms, or using UV sterilizers.

Aggression and Other Behavioral Problems

Like any animal, Koi can sometimes exhibit behavioral problems. Understanding these behaviors can help you manage them effectively:

Aggression: While Koi are generally peaceful, they can sometimes show aggression, especially during feeding times or when the pond is overcrowded. To mitigate this, ensure your pond is spacious enough for the number of Koi you have and consider separate feeding areas for larger or more dominant fish.

Overeating: Koi are known to eat whenever food is available, which can lead to overeating and related health problems. To prevent this, establish a regular feeding schedule and stick to it, providing only as much food as your fish can consume in a few minutes.

Unusual Swimming Patterns: If your Koi are swimming erratically or near the water's surface, this could indicate stress or illness. Check your water quality, monitor your fish for signs of disease, and consider consulting a Koi expert or vet for advice.

Addressing these common problems promptly and effectively can keep your Koi healthy and ensure they live a long and fulfilling life in your care.

Chapter 15: Koi Compatibility – Friend or Foe?

When creating a Koi pond, it's not just about the fish. Other elements of the ecosystem, including other fish, plants, and wildlife, play crucial roles in maintaining a healthy and balanced environment. However, not all species are compatible with Koi. This chapter will explore various aspects of Koi compatibility, from their interactions with other Koi to their relationship with plants and other pond inhabitants.

Koi and Other Koi:

Koi are generally social and peaceful fish that enjoy the company of their kind. They are often seen swimming together in groups, which is not just a beautiful sight but also a natural behavior for these gregarious fish.

Koi are widely revered for their calm and tranquil nature. These beautiful fish have a strong social structure and are inherently communal creatures. While some fish species are known to be solitary or aggressive towards their own kind, Koi are the exact opposite, making them a charming addition to any pond.

Observing a Koi pond, one of the most striking features is the sense of unity and harmony among the fish. Koi, regardless of their variety or color, are often seen swimming together in coordinated groups. This behavior, known as schooling, is a natural instinct for Koi. Schooling not only provides them with a sense of security from potential threats but also plays a crucial role in their social bonding and hierarchy.

When in a school, Koi tend to swim in the same direction at a similar speed, creating an enchanting, synchronized dance in the water. This formation also allows them to communicate more effectively with each other, whether for mating purposes or alerting others to food or potential danger.

However, it's important to note that while Koi are generally peaceful and enjoy each other's company, there are times when they might display territorial behaviors, especially during breeding season.

Male Koi may chase females, and sometimes other males, around the pond in an attempt to assert dominance. This is considered normal behavior and usually doesn't lead to harm.

Creating a well-balanced Koi community requires a basic understanding of their social behavior. Factors such as size, age, and variety can influence their social dynamics.

But fundamentally, Koi are social, peaceful fish that thrive in the company of their own kind, making them an ideal choice for those looking to create a serene and captivating pond environment.

Same-Species Compatibility:

While Koi fish have an inherent nature to coexist harmoniously with one another, certain factors can influence the dynamics of their interactions. One of these factors is the size of the Koi.

In a diverse group of Koi, it's likely that there will be some disparity in size. Larger Koi, due to their physical dominance, may sometimes bully smaller ones. This bullying isn't typically dangerous or life-threatening but can lead to stress among smaller fish and disrupt the otherwise peaceful pond environment.

In such cases, it's important for hobbyists to intervene. Bullying can be mitigated by ensuring that the pond is spacious enough for smaller fish to escape any potential bullies. It might also be useful to group Koi of similar sizes together, especially if the size difference is significant. Feeding larger Koi separately can also help ensure that smaller ones get their share of food.

Age is another factor that can impact the compatibility of Koi. Older Koi, which are usually larger and more settled, may not appreciate the high energy levels of younger, more active Koi. Younger Koi, full of vitality, might cause unnecessary stress to their older counterparts by constant chasing or nudging. Providing ample space and hiding spots can help in creating a peaceful environment for Koi of different ages.

Lastly, even within the same species, individual temperaments can vary. Some Koi might be naturally more assertive or territorial than others, especially during the breeding season. It's crucial for Koi keepers to closely observe their Koi's behavior, looking for any signs of aggression or stress.

Understanding these factors will enable hobbyists and Koi enthusiasts to ensure a harmonious living environment for their Koi. Creating such an environment contributes significantly to the overall well-being and longevity of these magnificent fish, allowing their full beauty and serene nature to shine through.

Size and Age Factors:

In the world of Koi keeping, one of the fundamental principles for maintaining a harmonious and stress-free pond is to consider the size and age of your Koi. While Koi are naturally social and often coexist peacefully, there are important reasons to group them with others of similar size and age.

Size Matters:

Keeping Koi of similar sizes together is crucial for several reasons:

- Reducing Competition: Koi are voracious eaters, and during feeding time, competition for food can become intense. Larger, more dominant Koi might outcompete smaller ones, leaving them underfed and stressed. By grouping Koi of similar sizes, you create a level playing field where all fish have an equal opportunity to feed.

- Minimizing Bullying: Larger Koi have the physical advantage to assert dominance over smaller ones. This can lead to bullying, which, while not usually dangerous, can cause stress and disrupt the tranquility of the pond.

When Koi of different sizes are mixed, it's essential to provide ample hiding spots or feeding areas where smaller Koi can retreat to avoid bullies.

- Balancing Growth: Koi grow at different rates, and placing them with similarly sized companions can help ensure that they all develop at a healthy pace. This avoids situations where one Koi significantly outgrows the others, which can create an imbalance in the pond's ecosystem.

Considering Age:
Age is another important factor to contemplate when grouping Koi:

- Energy Levels: Younger Koi tend to be more energetic and playful, which can sometimes disturb older, more placid Koi. By keeping Koi of similar ages together, you can avoid unnecessary stress and conflicts caused by differences in energy levels.
- Compatibility: Koi of similar ages are more likely to exhibit compatible behaviors. Younger Koi often engage in playful chasing and nudging, which can be stressful for

older, less active Koi. By grouping them by age, you can ensure that their behavior aligns more harmoniously.

Maintaining a Koi pond that promotes the well-being of your fish involves thoughtful consideration of size and age factors. Grouping Koi with similar sizes and ages helps minimize competition, reduce the likelihood of bullying, and create a balanced, serene environment where all your Koi have an equal opportunity to thrive and display their remarkable beauty.

Koi and Other Fish Species:

When considering introducing other fish species to your Koi pond, carefully assess their specific care requirements, potential for aggression, and impact on the existing pond ecosystem. It's advisable to consult with experienced Koi keepers or experts to ensure that the fish you choose will peacefully coexist with your cherished Koi and contribute positively to the overall well-being of your pond.

Koi can coexist peacefully with several other fish species. However, not all fish make good pond mates for Koi, and it's crucial to understand which species are compatible and which ones should be avoided.

Koi ponds can be dynamic ecosystems, and it's not uncommon for hobbyists to want to introduce other fish species to complement their Koi. However, not all fish make suitable companions for Koi, and it's essential to carefully consider compatibility to maintain a harmonious pond environment.

Common Pond Mates:

Common Pond Mates: Some of the most compatible species for Koi ponds include Goldfish and Plecostomus. Goldfish are closely related to Koi and share similar care requirements, while Plecostomus can help control algae and are generally peaceful.

When considering other fish species to coexist harmoniously with your Koi, it's essential to select compatible species that share similar care requirements and temperaments. Two of the most popular and compatible pond mates for Koi are Goldfish and Plecostomus.

Goldfish (Carassius auratus):
- Closely Related to Koi: Goldfish are closely related to Koi and belong to the same family (Cyprinidae). They share a common ancestor and thus have similar

requirements for water quality, temperature, and pH levels. This makes them ideal companions for Koi in a pond.

- Size and Variety: Goldfish come in various sizes and colors, offering a diverse and visually appealing addition to your pond. They can range from small and sleek Comet or Shubunkin Goldfish to larger and more ornate varieties like the Fantail or Oranda Goldfish.

- Peaceful Nature: Goldfish are generally peaceful fish, and their docile nature aligns well with the tranquility that Koi ponds often aim to create. They rarely exhibit aggressive behaviors that could disrupt the peaceful coexistence of your pond.

- Complementary Aesthetics: The combination of colorful Koi and various Goldfish varieties creates a stunning visual display in your pond. The contrasting colors and patterns of these fish can be a captivating sight.

- Hardiness: Goldfish are known for their hardiness, making them resilient and adaptable to changing pond conditions. This makes them suitable for novice pond keepers as well as seasoned enthusiasts.

Plecostomus (Plecostomus spp.):
- Algae Control: Plecostomus, often referred to as "suckerfish" or "algae eaters," are valuable additions to a Koi pond. They have a voracious appetite for algae and help maintain water quality by keeping algae growth in check. Their algae-eating habits contribute to a cleaner and clearer pond.

- Peaceful Behavior: Plecostomus are known for their peaceful disposition. They rarely engage in aggressive behaviors and are unlikely to disturb the harmony of your pond. They are also nocturnal, so their activity is primarily at night.

- Compatibility with Koi: Plecostomus are compatible with Koi because they inhabit different areas of the pond. Plecos tend to stay near the bottom, while Koi swim in various water depths. This reduces the likelihood of direct competition for resources.

- Variety: There are several species and varieties of Plecostomus available, each with its unique appearance. Common species include the Common Pleco (Hypostomus plecostomus) and the Bristlenose Pleco (Ancistrus spp.).

- Maintenance: While Plecostomus can help control algae, it's important to note that they require supplementary food, as algae alone may not provide sufficient nutrition. Provide them with sinking algae wafers or pellets to ensure their well-being.

Incorporating Goldfish and Plecostomus into your Koi pond can enhance its aesthetics, improve water quality, and contribute to a more balanced ecosystem. However, it's essential to monitor the compatibility and ensure that the pond's size and filtration can support the additional fish. Regular observation and proper care will help maintain a healthy and harmonious pond environment for all its inhabitants.

- White Amur (Grass Carp): If your pond has issues with excessive aquatic plant growth, White Amur can be a natural solution. They are herbivorous and can help control the spread of unwanted aquatic plants. Be cautious about introducing them, though, as they grow large and require adequate space.

- Rosy Red Minnows: These small, hardy fish can serve as both companions and live food for Koi. They are prolific breeders and can provide entertainment for your Koi as they chase them around.

Species to Avoid:

Certain species should not be kept with Koi. For instance, aggressive or territorial fish, like some types of Cichlids, can stress or harm Koi. Similarly, fish that prefer significantly different water parameters may not thrive in a Koi pond.

While there are many suitable companions for Koi in a pond, it's equally crucial to be aware of fish species that should be avoided. Introducing incompatible or aggressive species can lead to stress, harm, or even the death of your Koi. Here are some types of fish that are generally best kept away from Koi ponds:

While some fish can coexist harmoniously with Koi, there are others that are not recommended due to various reasons:

Aggressive or Territorial Fish:

- Cichlids: Many Cichlid species are known for their territorial and aggressive behaviors. They can harass and stress out Koi, which are generally peaceful by nature. Moreover, Cichlids often prefer different water conditions, making them unsuitable companions for Koi.

- Aggressive Tropical Fish: Some aggressive tropical fish, like certain types of Barbs or African Cichlids, are not compatible with Koi due to their aggressive tendencies. These fish can harass and potentially harm your Koi, leading to injuries or even fatalities.

Fish with Different Water Parameter Requirements:

- Tropical Fish: Most tropical fish species require warmer water temperatures than Koi, which prefer cooler water. Mixing tropical fish with Koi can result in suboptimal conditions for both groups. Additionally, tropical fish may have different pH and hardness requirements that don't align with Koi's needs.

- Saltwater Fish: The saltwater requirements of marine fish make them entirely incompatible with freshwater Koi. Mixing saltwater fish with Koi would be detrimental to both groups due to the stark differences in salinity and water chemistry.

Invasive or Non-Native Species:
- Invasive Species: Introducing non-native or invasive fish species into your pond can have severe ecological consequences. These species can outcompete and harm native aquatic life, disrupt the natural balance of your pond, and even lead to ecological damage in local waterways if they escape.

Fin-Nipping or Harassing Fish:
- Fish that Nip or Harass: Certain species, like some types of Barbs or Tetras, are notorious for being fin nippers. They may relentlessly nip at the fins of Koi, causing stress and potential health problems. Such interactions can lead to injury and vulnerability to disease.

Large Predatory Fish:

- Large Predators: Species of fish that grow to a substantial size and are predatory by nature, such as large catfish or predatory pike, can pose a significant threat to Koi. These fish can prey on Koi, leading to a considerable loss of prized fish.

When considering fish to coexist with your Koi, always research the specific needs, behaviors, and compatibility of potential additions. Avoid introducing fish that are known to be aggressive, territorial, or have significantly different water parameter requirements. Ensuring compatibility is crucial for maintaining a serene and balanced pond environment, allowing your Koi to thrive in a stress-free setting.

Koi and Aquatic Plants:

Keeping live plants in a Koi pond can provide numerous benefits, including oxygenation, filtration, and natural food sources. However, Koi are known for their plant-eating habits, which can pose challenges.

Incorporating aquatic plants into your Koi pond can create a stunning and naturalistic aquatic environment while offering several benefits, including improved water quality, oxygenation, and natural food sources. However, the plant-eating habits of Koi can pose both challenges and opportunities for successful coexistence between Koi and aquatic plants.

Benefits and Challenges:

While plants can contribute to water quality and provide cover and spawning sites, Koi may uproot or consume certain varieties. This can damage or even destroy the plants and disrupt the pond's aesthetics.

The incorporation of aquatic plants into a Koi pond offers a range of benefits, but it also presents certain challenges. This section explores both the advantages and potential difficulties associated with maintaining aquatic plants in a Koi pond.

Benefits of Aquatic Plants in a Koi Pond:

- Water Quality Improvement: Aquatic plants play a crucial role in enhancing water quality. They absorb excess nutrients, such as ammonia and nitrates, from the water, effectively acting as a natural filtration system. This nutrient uptake helps prevent algae blooms and keeps the water clear and healthy for Koi.

- Oxygenation: Through photosynthesis, aquatic plants release oxygen into the water. This additional oxygen benefits Koi by supporting their respiratory needs and promoting overall pond health.

- Shade and Cover: Aquatic plants provide shade, which is particularly beneficial during hot weather. Koi can seek refuge from direct sunlight beneath the plants, reducing stress and the risk of overheating. Additionally, the dense foliage of aquatic plants serves as a hiding place, offering Koi protection from potential predators.

- Spawning Sites: Many aquatic plants create suitable spawning sites for Koi. The plants' leaves and roots provide a safe environment for Koi fry to develop, reducing the risk of predation.

Challenges of Aquatic Plants in a Koi Pond:

- Plant-Eating Behavior: Koi are notorious plant eaters. Their grazing can lead to the uprooting and consumption of aquatic plants. Certain Koi may exhibit more voracious plant-eating habits than others, potentially damaging or even destroying the plants in the process.

- Selective Feeding: Koi often display selective feeding behavior, favoring some aquatic plant varieties while ignoring others. This can result in uneven plant growth and aesthetics, with certain types of plants thriving while others struggle.

- Aesthetics and Maintenance: Koi's plant-eating habits can disrupt the pond's aesthetics, as uprooted or damaged plants may need frequent replacement or repositioning. This can increase maintenance efforts and costs.

Creating a Balance:

To strike a balance between the benefits of aquatic plants and the challenges posed by Koi, consider the following strategies:

- Plant Selection: Choose plant varieties that are less palatable to Koi. Research and select hardy species that have a higher likelihood of coexisting peacefully with your Koi.

- Protective Measures: Implement physical barriers or planting containers to shield delicate plants from Koi. This can prevent them from being uprooted or consumed.

- Feeding Routine: Ensure that your Koi receive a well-balanced diet to reduce their reliance on aquatic plants for nutrition. High-quality Koi pellets and supplemental treats can help satisfy their dietary needs.

- Regular Monitoring: Continuously assess the condition of both your aquatic plants and your Koi. Adjust your approach as necessary to maintain a harmonious balance between them.

The presence of aquatic plants in a Koi pond offers numerous advantages in terms of water quality, aesthetics, and Koi health. While Koi's plant-eating habits can present challenges, these can be effectively managed through careful plant selection, protective measures, and proper feeding practices. When successfully balanced, aquatic plants can contribute significantly to the overall well-being of both your Koi and your pond environment.

Recommended Plants:

Some plants are more resilient or less appealing to Koi and are thus better suited for a Koi pond. These include water lilies, iris, and cattails, among others.

In a Koi pond, selecting the right aquatic plants is crucial to strike a balance between creating a visually appealing environment, improving water quality, and accommodating the plant-eating habits of Koi. Here, we explore several plant varieties that are known to be more resilient or less appealing to Koi, making them suitable choices for a Koi pond.

1. Water Lilies (Nymphaea spp.):
   - Resilient: Water lilies are a popular choice for Koi ponds because they are known for their resilience. Their sturdy leaves and floating flowers can withstand occasional Koi nibbling.

   - Shade and Aesthetics: Water lilies provide valuable shade, reducing stress on Koi during hot weather. Their beautiful blooms add a stunning visual element to the pond.

2. Iris (Iris spp.):

- Hardy: Irises are hardy aquatic plants that can tolerate Koi grazing. They feature tall, slender stems with striking, sword-like leaves.

- Natural Filtration: Irises contribute to water quality by helping to absorb excess nutrients. Their dense root systems act as natural filters.

3. Cattails (Typha spp.):

- Beneficial and Tough: Cattails are robust and can withstand Koi activity. They contribute to water quality by absorbing nutrients and providing oxygen.

- Habitat for Wildlife: Cattails offer habitat and food sources for various pond wildlife, enhancing the overall ecosystem.

4. Anacharis (Elodea canadensis):

- Fast Growth: Anacharis is a fast-growing submerged plant that can outpace Koi consumption. It's often used to oxygenate the water and provide cover for fry.

- Low Maintenance: Anacharis is relatively low maintenance and can thrive in a Koi pond without much fuss.

5. Water Hyacinth (Eichhornia crassipes):
- Floating Beauty: Water hyacinth features attractive floating foliage and lavender-blue flowers. It can help shade Koi and reduce sunlight penetration, minimizing algae growth.

- Nutrient Uptake: Water hyacinth is known for its nutrient-absorbing capabilities, aiding in water quality management.

6. Horsetail (Equisetum hyemale):
- Tough and Resilient: Horsetail is a hardy, reed-like plant with jointed stems. Its toughness makes it a good choice for Koi ponds.

- Architectural Appeal: Horsetail adds architectural interest to the pond with its unique appearance.

7. Japanese Sweet Flag (Acorus gramineus):

- Grassy Aesthetic: Japanese sweet flag resembles ornamental grass and can lend a graceful, grassy look to the pond's margins.

- Tolerant of Grazing: While not entirely immune to Koi nibbling, Japanese sweet flag can withstand some level of grazing.

8. Pickerelweed (Pontederia cordata):
- Colorful Blooms: Pickerelweed boasts vibrant purple-blue flower spikes that add a splash of color to the pond.

- Tall Growth: Its tall stems can sometimes deter Koi from reaching the leaves, preserving the plant's appearance.

When selecting aquatic plants for your Koi pond, consider a mix of these recommended varieties to ensure a balance between aesthetics, water quality, and Koi well-being. Keep in mind that while these plants are more resilient, monitoring and maintenance are still essential to create a thriving and harmonious pond environment.

Koi and Other Pond Life:

Koi typically coexist peacefully with a variety of other pond life, including frogs, snails, and certain types of crustaceans. However, it's important to monitor interactions to ensure all creatures are cohabiting harmoniously.

Koi ponds are dynamic ecosystems that can host a variety of aquatic life beyond just Koi. This section explores the interactions between Koi and other pond inhabitants, such as frogs, snails, and certain crustaceans. While Koi typically coexist peacefully with these creatures, careful monitoring and consideration are necessary to ensure a harmonious pond environment.

1. Frogs:
- Natural Pond Inhabitants: Frogs are often naturally drawn to Koi ponds due to the availability of water, shelter, and food sources. They can contribute to the overall ecosystem and are a sign of a healthy pond.
- Beneficial Predators: Frogs are beneficial as they consume insects and pests that may otherwise bother your Koi. Their presence can help control mosquito larvae and other aquatic pests.

- Monitoring Interaction: While frogs and Koi generally coexist peacefully, there may be occasional interactions. Koi may nibble on frog eggs or tadpoles, and frogs might be attracted to Koi pellets. Observing their interactions can help ensure both species thrive.

2. Snails:
- Algae Control: Snails, such as pond snails, can contribute to algae control by grazing on algae growth on pond surfaces and plants. They help maintain water clarity.
- Minimal Interaction: Snails typically have minimal interaction with Koi. Koi may occasionally investigate snails, but they are generally uninterested in them as a food source.
- Population Control: Be mindful of snail populations. While they can be beneficial, an overabundance of snails can become a nuisance. Consider introducing snail-eating fish or manually removing excess snails if necessary.

3. Crustaceans (e.g., Crayfish):
- Bottom Dwellers: Crustaceans like crayfish often inhabit the pond's bottom areas. They are generally unobtrusive

and do not interfere with Koi swimming in the open water.

- Algae and Debris Cleanup: Crustaceans contribute to the ecosystem by scavenging and consuming organic matter on the pond's bottom, helping to maintain water quality.
- Size Matters: Crustaceans vary in size, and it's essential to choose species that won't pose a threat to Koi. Larger crayfish, for example, are less likely to be pursued by Koi.

Harmonious Coexistence:

To ensure harmonious coexistence between Koi and other pond life:

- Monitor Interaction: Regularly observe the interactions between Koi and other pond inhabitants. This allows you to address any issues promptly.

- Provide Hiding Places: Offering hiding places, such as rocks, plants, or structures, can give smaller creatures a refuge from Koi and reduce stress.

- Maintain Water Quality: Ensure optimal water quality to support the health of all pond inhabitants. Proper filtration, water testing, and maintenance are essential.

- Control Population: Keep an eye on the population of other pond life, such as snails or crayfish. If their numbers become excessive, consider population control measures.

Understanding Koi compatibility is crucial for maintaining a peaceful and balanced pond ecosystem. It's not just about mixing different species but creating an environment where all inhabitants can thrive. Compatibility extends beyond just fish—it's about the entire pond community and ensuring every element contributes positively to the overall health and harmony of your pond.

Chapter 16: The Business of Koi

The beauty and popularity of Koi fish present numerous business opportunities for enthusiasts. Here are some areas of specialization or business types that one can consider:

Koi Breeding: Koi breeding is one of the most common areas of specialization. As a breeder, you would maintain a selection of high-quality Koi, breed them, and sell the offspring to other hobbyists or retailers.

Koi Retail: If you have the ability to source high-quality Koi but are not interested in breeding yourself, you could start a Koi retail business. This involves purchasing Koi from breeders (either domestic or overseas) and selling them to the end consumer.

Pond Design and Construction: Many Koi keepers prefer to have professionally designed and constructed ponds. If you have knowledge and skills in landscaping and construction, you could specialize in designing and building Koi ponds.

Pond Maintenance Services: Koi ponds require regular maintenance, including water testing, cleaning, and equipment checks. Offering a professional maintenance service can be a profitable venture.

Koi Health Consultation: If you have substantial knowledge about Koi health and disease management, you could offer consultation services to other Koi keepers. This might include diagnosing and treating sick Koi, as well as providing preventative care advice.

Koi Food and Supplies: Selling Koi food, pond equipment, and other related supplies is another potential business opportunity. This could be a brick-and-mortar store, an online shop, or both.

Koi Shows and Events: Organizing Koi shows and events can be an exciting way to immerse yourself in the world of Koi while also earning income. This requires substantial organization and planning skills.

Koi Information Services: If you have expert knowledge about Koi and enjoy sharing that knowledge, you could write books, create an informational website or blog, start a YouTube channel, or offer classes and workshops about Koi keeping.

Koi Pond Accessories: Specializing in the manufacture or sale of Koi pond accessories can also be a profitable niche. These could include items such as decorative bridges, statues, water features, lighting fixtures, or seating arrangements specifically designed for Koi ponds.

Koi Photography and Art: Koi are known for their beauty and grace, making them excellent subjects for photography and art. If you have skills in these areas, you could sell your Koi-themed artworks or offer professional photography services for Koi owners who want high-quality images of their fish.

You could also provide photographs for Koi-related magazines, websites, or promotional materials.

Koi Travel Tours: If you live in a region renowned for its Koi culture or if there are various high-profile Koi ponds in your area, you could organize Koi-themed travel tours.

This could appeal to both local and international Koi enthusiasts who want to explore prominent Koi destinations.

Aquatic Plants Specialist: Koi ponds often feature a variety of aquatic plants, both for their aesthetic contribution and their role in maintaining a healthy pond ecosystem. A business centered around selling these plants and advising on their care and use in Koi ponds could be a valuable niche.

Koi Pond Filtration Systems: Designing, selling, and installing advanced filtration systems for Koi ponds is another business possibility. Specialized systems can enhance the water quality and overall health of the Koi.

Koi Rescue Services: Unfortunately, there can be situations where Koi are not properly cared for, or where an owner can no longer maintain their pond. A Koi rescue service could take in these fish, provide them with the necessary care, and then rehome them to suitable environments.

Koi App Development: If you have tech skills, you could create an app related to Koi keeping. This might include features like a disease diagnostic tool, reminders for pond maintenance tasks, a platform for buying and selling Koi, or even a social networking feature for Koi enthusiasts to connect and share advice.

Koi-themed Merchandise: If you have a creative streak, you could create and sell Koi-themed merchandise. This might include items such as T-shirts, mugs, wall art, or jewelry featuring Koi designs.

Koi Auctions: An online platform where breeders can auction their Koi to the highest bidder could be a unique business model that brings together Koi breeders and enthusiasts from all over the world.

As always, the success of these business ventures would depend on careful planning, understanding the market, and delivering a high-quality product or service. With the right approach, they could be a great way to turn a love for Koi into a profitable business.

Chapter 17: Joining the Koi Community

The importance of community cannot be overstated, especially in a niche hobby like Koi keeping. Becoming part of a Koi community provides support, learning opportunities, and camaraderie. This chapter aims to guide you on how to join and get involved in Koi communities, both locally and online, and also introduces the exciting world of Koi shows and competitions.

Importance of Community

Keeping Koi is a rewarding but complex hobby. Joining a Koi community can help mitigate some of the challenges you might face along the way. It provides a platform for you to connect with other enthusiasts, share experiences, ask questions, and learn from the collective knowledge of the group.

These communities are filled with members ranging from novices to seasoned experts who are usually eager to assist one another.

Furthermore, being part of a Koi community can also provide opportunities to buy, sell, or trade Koi and equipment. Members often share information about the best local suppliers, upcoming sales, or they might offer their own surplus supplies or fish at discounted prices.

Local Koi Clubs

Check if there's a local Koi club in your area. These clubs typically hold regular meetings, seminars, pond tours, and social events. They offer great opportunities for networking, learning from experienced members, and seeing a variety of Koi ponds firsthand.

Online Koi Communities:

In the digital age, there are numerous online forums, social media groups, and websites dedicated to Koi keeping where advice and support are available 24/7. These platforms allow you to connect with a wider, more diverse group of Koi enthusiasts from around the world.

Koi Shows and Competitions

Koi shows and competitions are major events in the Koi community. They are places where breeders and enthusiasts showcase their Koi, judged by strict criteria including body shape, color, pattern, and overall condition.

Participating in or attending these shows not only provides a chance to see some of the best Koi, but also to learn about high standards in Koi care and breeding.Joining the Koi community can enrich your Koi keeping journey significantly. It offers countless learning and social opportunities, and it can provide invaluable support as you delve deeper into the world of Koi.

Chapter 18: Koi Hobbyist vs. Koi Businessman

The world of Koi keeping is diverse, encompassing both hobbyists and businessmen. While they both share a love for these ornamental fish, their motivations, methods, and measures of success can differ significantly.

A Koi hobbyist is someone who keeps Koi for personal enjoyment and fulfillment. They are drawn by the allure of Koi's mesmerizing colors and patterns, their graceful movements, and the tranquility they bring to any garden. Koi hobbyists often find themselves captivated by the aesthetic appeal of a Koi pond and the opportunity to observe and interact with these remarkable creatures.

For the Koi hobbyist, it's all about the love of Koi and the joy of maintaining a healthy, vibrant pond. They're not motivated by monetary gain but by the intrinsic value of the hobby itself—the serenity it brings, the connection with nature it provides, and the satisfaction derived from caring for these living works of art

.

To the Koi hobbyist, the hours spent tending to their Koi pond, feeding their fish, and learning about Koi health and maintenance are considered leisure time. This is a peaceful retreat from the demands of everyday life, an opportunity to relax, engage with nature, and enjoy the company of their fish.

For hobbyists, the journey is just as important as the destination. They appreciate the learning process and are open to the trial and error that comes with mastering Koi keeping. Whether it's understanding the intricacies of Koi diet and nutrition, identifying and treating diseases, or navigating the challenges of pond maintenance, each experience is an opportunity for growth and increased knowledge.

A Koi businessman, however, approaches Koi keeping from a different angle. For them, it's not merely a hobby—it's a business venture. Their primary goal is to make a profit from selling Koi or related products and services.

Koi businessmen must consider factors such as cost-effectiveness, market demand, and scalability in their operations. Every decision—from which Koi breeds to invest in, to the type of pond setup to use—is made with an eye on profitability and business growth.

Businessmen often scale up their operations over time. They may start with a single pond, but as the business grows, so too might the number of ponds and the variety of Koi they keep. Additionally, they might expand their business to include related services, such as pond design and installation, Koi healthcare, or selling Koi keeping supplies.

To run a successful Koi business, a deep understanding of Koi keeping is necessary—going beyond what a hobbyist might typically know. This includes expert knowledge on breeding Koi, controlling diseases, understanding market trends, and knowing how to meet customer demands effectively.

Some hobbyists may decide to turn their passion for Koi keeping into a business. This transition requires careful consideration and planning. This section will guide readers on how to assess their readiness, navigate potential challenges, and seize opportunities to establish a successful Koi business.

Whether one is a Koi hobbyist or a Koi businessman, the underlying love for these fascinating creatures is the common ground. Understanding the differences between these two roles can offer valuable insights, whether you're considering embarking on your Koi keeping journey or contemplating turning a beloved hobby into a business venture.

Made in United States
Orlando, FL
15 June 2024

47930789R00059